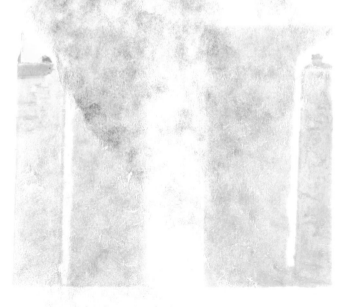

How Can I Help?
Friends Helping Friends™

HELPING A FRIEND WITH AN EATING DISORDER

Sabrina Parys

ROSEN
PUBLISHING

New York

Published in 2017 by The Rosen Publishing Group, Inc.
29 East 21st Street, New York, NY 10010

Library of Congress Cataloging-in-Publication Data

Names: Parys, Sabrina, author.
Title: Helping a friend with an eating disorder / Sabrina Parys.
Description: First edition. | New York : Rosen Publishing, 2017. | Series: How can I help? Friends helping friends | Includes bibliographical references and index.
Identifiers: LCCN 2016017674| ISBN 9781499464351 (library bound) | ISBN 9781508171898 (paperback) | ISBN 9781508171904 (6-pack)
Subjects: LCSH: Eating disorders—Juvenile literature. | Eating disorders—Social aspects—Juvenile literature. | Eating disorders—Treatment—Juvenile literature.
Classification: LCC RC552.E18 P37 2017 | DDC 616.85/2600835—dc23
LC record available at https://lccn.loc.gov/2016017674.

Manufactured in China

CONTENTS

INTRODUCTION

Y ou and a friend are walking one afternoon and you can't stop thinking about a rumor you heard at school. A few people in your class walked in on your friend vomiting in the bathroom, and now they think she has an eating disorder. You want to ask her if this is true—not all rumors are, after all. You would like to believe it to be false. The signs point toward the negative: your friend doesn't look emaciated, she doesn't seem to avoid food, and she doesn't seem depressed. But what if the rumor is true? You want to ask—she's your best friend and you would do anything for her. Has she been going through this disorder right before your eyes? How can this be? If it is true, how could you help her?

At some point during adolescence, many teenagers are likely to meet someone with an eating disorder. Yet for a variety of reasons, a person suffering from one might not share his or her struggle with others. According to the National Eating Disorders Association (NEDA), at least 20 million women and 10 million men will be affected by an eating disorder during their lifetime. Eating disorders can happen to anyone. However, teenagers and young adults are more likely to experience one: 95 percent of those currently affected by an eating disorder are between the ages of 12 and 25, according to the National Association of Anorexia Nervosa and Associated Disorders (ANAD).

Struggling with one's body image is tough, especially during adolescence, when the body undergoes constant

Many teenagers find themselves comparing their growing bodies to the unrealistic and limited beauty standards that the media perpetuates.

change, and the lack of diversity in the media can lead many teens to believe in an unrealistic body image. However, a common misconception about disordered eating is that the disease is all about food. The fact is, disordered eating is usually symptomatic of larger, underlying issues with psychological roots. Bullying, body shaming, limited access to mental health care, poor self-esteem, and abuse are just a few experiences that can contribute to harmful dietary habits.

The bigger problem with eating disorders is not just that they can (and do) take a toll on one's health, but also that they can happen right before our eyes, every day. Eating disorders are often silent and can be invisible, with those closest to the person missing the signs all along. There are many ways that eating disorders can be prevented or treated, but early recognition is the key to most successful recoveries.

Although it may not always be obvious when someone is struggling with an eating disorder, there are steps that you can take to recognize early warning signs and help a friend who is exhibiting them. Confronting someone you love about an eating disorder might feel awkward or nerve-wracking. It is never easy to watch someone you care about suffer. However, you are not powerless. If you sense a friend might be developing or has developed an eating disorder, there are many ways that you can help.

CHAPTER ONE

UNDERSTANDING EATING DISORDERS

S o, you suspect that your friend might have an eating disorder. As it happens, misconceptions can lead to misperceptions. Just because you see your friend skip out on lunch once does not mean he or she is suffering from one, but there are signs that can help you determine if there is a problem.

WHAT ARE EATING DISORDERS?

Eating disorders are incredibly complex conditions characterized by unhealthy eating patterns. They have a harmful impact on one's physical and mental health, which increases if left untreated. They can span a wide range of behaviors, including restriction, bingeing, purging, and even compulsive exercising. Because eating disorders are so varied, these abnormal dieting behaviors—and the reasons behind them—can shift, overlap, and develop through time.

However, it is important to learn the difference between disordered behavior and an interest in health in order to differentiate between the two. The Mayo Clinic rec-

A compulsive or excessive preoccupation with food that interferes with everyday functioning can be a sign of an eating disorder.

ommends that children above the age of six get at least one hour of rigorous exercise per day and eat a balanced diet filled with grains, vegetables, fruits, proteins, and dairy. So it is perfectly normal—even encouraged—for teenagers and young adults to be active and take an interest in the food they choose to consume.

If you notice a friend has begun to focus on eating healthy or has started an exercise regimen, this does not necessarily mean that he or she is exhibiting symptoms of disordered eating. Healthy life habits are good to cultivate, especially for growing bodies. It is only when these interests take on an obsessive quality, affecting one's everyday behavior and health, that there is reason for concern.

SPOT THE DIFFERENCE: ALTERNATIVE DIETS VS. DISORDERED EATING

It can be hard to spot the difference between disordered eating and an alternative diet, but it is important to know what separates a practice from a problem. Sometimes belief systems, health crises, or ethical dilemmas can make a diet seem abnormal. But this does not mean that those involved in specific dietary practices are participating in destructive dietary habits.

The religion a person follows can dictate what his or her diet consists of, making certain food or products

(continue on the next page)

(continued from the previous page)

off-limits or discouraged. For instance, most Muslims abstain from eating pork products, and many practicing Buddhists eat vegetarian diets. Medical problems or dietary intolerances can also play a role in food consumption. An individual with celiac disease, for example, cannot process gluten, a protein found in wheat and many bread products. As a result, gluten-free products must take the place of agitators that can cause illness.

There are also many people who choose to eat a meatless and/or dairy-free diet because of their ethical objections to animal treatment and consumption. These vegetarians and vegans can supplement their diets with specialized products to get the nutrients they need. As long as the above practices do not coexist with an alarming preoccupation with body image, weight, or food, an alternative diet can be perfectly healthy, normal, and, indeed, very common.

WHY DO EATING DISORDERS HAPPEN?

All too often, people treat eating disorders as phases or lifestyle choices. You may hear someone talk about these conditions as if they were no big deal. "Oh, she'll get over it," or "That's just the way he eats." But nonchalant language can cover up the seriousness of a problem. What many people fail to consider is that eating disorders rarely resolve themselves without outside intervention. Indeed, they are just as complex as people who suffer from them. In fact, two people with the same eating disorder may have developed it for completely different reasons. Medical professionals agree that disordered eating can be caused by biological, psychological, societal, or even environmental factors.

Helping a friend with an eating disorder can be challenging, but taking the time to learn about why these diseases arise may help you to understand the challenges your friend might be facing.

BIOLOGICAL FACTORS

Researchers are exploring how our biology can influence the development of eating disorders. Some studies hypothesize that eating disorders may have some basis in genetics and can sometimes be inherited. Functional magnetic resonance imaging (fMRI) studies, medical imaging used to watch brain activity, have shown that the brain of a patient experiencing anorexia fails to acknowledge the body's need for nutrition. For reasons such as these, it can be difficult for a patient to think logically about his or her condition and about a healthy relationship with food.

PSYCHOLOGY

For many individuals, eating disorders arise as coping mechanisms or as the result of psychological trauma. Teenagers who experience other mental health issues such as anxiety or depression may also develop eating disorders as a way to

A lack of diversity in media leads many teenagers to assume that their bodies should look a certain way, causing them to develop a negative body image.

avoid stress in other parts of life. Being bullied throughout childhood about one's appearance or weight can lead to a negative body image and low self-esteem. Likewise, bullying that occurs on social media can have damaging affects on the way people perceive themselves.

Growing up in a household where looking a certain way was modeled and stressed can lead some people to expect the same of themselves. Also, those who have had unstable upbringings or have experienced verbal abuse may have learned to use food as a source of control or comfort.

SOCIETY AND ENVIRONMENT

It is no secret that our society still struggles with representations of a healthy body image. It can seem like everywhere you look, thinness is glorified and connected to the idea of health. Although media have made some small strides to tackle these issues in recent years, the overwhelming lack of diversity can be frustrating because it sets a standard that is so far removed from what real life and real bodies look like. When magazines Photoshop their models, they continue to perpetuate this ideal even further. It is no wonder that many individuals find themselves comparing their bodies to the ones they have been trained to treat as standards of perfection. The overwhelming pressure many people feel to live up to these images can cause some people to pursue unhealthy diets, which unfortunately, for many, can also lead to disordered eating.

Other aspects of a social environment can also play a serious role in eating disorder development. Competitive activities such as sports or modeling can sometimes require a high level of fitness and, in some cases, weight management. For people who are active in such environments, it can be easy to fall into the trap of unhealthy dieting. Likewise, being surrounded by negative examples of diet or food choice in the home or with friends can lead someone into disordered eating.

WHO DO EATING DISORDERS AFFECT?

A common misconception of eating disorders that still persists is that they only affect upper-middle class white

While many competitive sports and arts put pressure on participants to watch their diet, no activity is worth encouraging the development of an eating disorder.

females in their teens and twenties. Yet, research is rapidly destroying that stereotype. Eating disorders do not discriminate: they can affect any person from any race, class, gender, sexual orientation, and age. It is dangerous to fall into the trap of believing someone might not have an eating disorder because they do not "seem" to fit the stereotype for one. Recent studies have shown that certain cultural and societal pressures can also contribute to the development of eating disorders within the LGBTQ community, within the African American community, in males, and even in elderly populations.

MYTHS AND FACTS

MYTH: People with eating disorders are attention seekers.

FACT: Eating disorders are both physical and psychological in nature, so they are not choices or phases. Those who have one often alter their clothes, actions, and relationships to avoid drawing attention to themselves.

MYTH: You can tell if someone has an eating disorder by a person's appearance.

FACT: Extreme thinness or emaciation are signs of an eating disorder, but are not always present. Eating disorders manifest themselves in many ways.

MYTH: When people with an eating disorder gain back the weight they lost or lose the weight they gained, they have overcome their disorder.

FACT: Eating disorders are much more than changes in weight. Recovery is deeply rooted in learning how to cultivate a positive relationship with food, the mind, and one's environment.

CHAPTER TWO

TYPES OF EATING DISORDERS AND THEIR SYMPTOMS

Eating disorders come in many forms and can thus be recognized by their different symptoms. Although it can be difficult to know what disordered eating looks like, educating yourself about accompanying symptoms—both invisible and visible—is a necessary first step in learning how to help a friend who may be suffering from one.

ANOREXIA NERVOSA

Anorexia nervosa, or anorexia, is an eating disorder that is defined by a severe reduction of calorie intake resulting in a low body weight and starvation. It predominantly affects young women during adolescence, and according to NEDA results in death in 5–20 percent of known cases. Those suffering with anorexia often exhibit an intense fear of weight gain. If not treated early, the disorder can result in dramatic and even deadly weight loss.

While restriction, or eating sparsely, may be the main method of weight control for these individuals, many other

Restriction (severely limiting the amount of food ingested) is a dangerous and habit-forming type of weight control that can be a part of anorexia. It's also thought of as a separate eating disorder.

compensatory tactics are often used to ensure that weight is not gained. Sufferers may purge, or induce vomiting, after any small intake of food; obsess about calorie counting and weighing in; abuse laxatives, diuretics, or diet pills; and even exercise in excess to burn off any perceived weight gain.

When dealing with anorexia, it is important to note that those affected by the disease can take pride in their ability to control their diet. Sufferers can become reluctant about maintaining a normal weight or body mass index (BMI) and often deny the severity of their condition.

BULIMIA NERVOSA

Unlike anorexia, bulimia nervosa can be difficult to detect because it does not always result in dramatic weight loss.

Those who suffer from bulimia are interested in maintaining their weight. But this takes place through a dangerous cycle of bingeing and purging, or bingeing and restriction. Individuals participate in episodes of overeating and tend to consume large quantities of calorie-rich food quickly and secretly. During binges, individuals often feel as though they have no control, and sessions are often followed by intense regret, depression, panic, and various attempts to prevent weight gain.

While bulimia is most often associated with self-induced vomiting, it is also not uncommon for participants to engage in compensatory behavior such as severe food restriction in order to make up for calories consumed. Like anorexia, binge eating can also be marked by the use of diuretics, fasting, compulsive exercise, and laxative abuse in order to "cancel out" the calories consumed during binges.

BINGE EATING

Binge eating disorder (BED) is the most prevalent eating disorder in the United States. The Binge Eating Disorder Association (BEDA) reports that 3.5 percent of women and 2 percent of men have been clinically diagnosed with this disorder.

What differentiates BED from anorexia or bulimia is that individuals usually do not engage in compensatory behavior, such as purging or starvation. The *Diagnostic and Statistical Manual of Mental Disorders (DSM-5)*, a guide used by the American Psychiatric Association (APA) to classify mental illnesses, defines binge eaters as engaging in the following behaviors: repeated episodes of binge eating at least once a week during a three-month period; the consumption of food in excess during any given meal period;

DANGEROUS DIETING CULTURE: DEMYSTIFYING FADS AND OTHER DIETING MYTHS

Contrary to what many teens might think, dieting should not be a normal part of the adolescent experience. Although there are exceptions to this rule, which may include a medical condition or a doctor-approved dietary plan, teens should always think twice and consult a physician before undertaking any weight-loss endeavor on their own. Many popular websites, articles, or TV shows make dieting seem like a fun or necessary thing to do, but this is far from the truth. Teens should be wary of sources that endorse practices such as cleansing, diet pills, juice diets, fasting, or selective eating as methods guaranteeing dramatic weight loss. Many of these diet programs are fad diets, or diets that are unhealthy, unsustainable, and not approved by the medical community. Struggling with image can be tough, especially during adolescence when the body is undergoing constant change, but eating healthily, exercising in moderation, and being honest with your physician is really the best way to respect your body as it continues to grow.

and feeling little to no control over the amount of food one eats. People suffering from BED continue to eat even when full and often eat alone and quickly.

OTHER SPECIFIED FEEDING OR EATING DISORDERS (OSFED)

Many people who struggle with an eating disorder may not fit all of the criteria of one specific type. In fact, many people can suffer with some aspect of disordered eating their entire life without getting help — and these disorders can be just as serious and deadly.

OSFED, or other specified feeding or eating disorders, is a category created by the DSM-5 to expand upon the pre-existing term of EDNOS, or eating disorder not otherwise specified. These terms exist so that people who exhibit symptoms of atypical disorders can receive the help they need without being turned away by doctors. For example, someone can exhibit symptoms of anorexia without being underweight, and another person can exhibit symptoms of bulimia without binge eating every day, yet their abnormal dieting behaviors are still cause for concern and treatment.

VISIBLE VS. INVISIBLE SYMPTOMS— UNDERSTANDING THE DIFFERENCE

Unusual, secretive behavior or dramatic changes in the body are often the first signs that a friend might have an eating disorder. Yet sometimes the symptoms can be invisible and difficult to see. Individuals who are developing or have developed an eating disorder can be especially conscious of their appearance, behavior, and language, and may take extreme precautions in order to avoid drawing unwanted attention to themselves. However, it is still possible for others to discern that something is not right.

THE VISIBLE: BEHAVIORAL AND PHYSICAL

In cases where restrictive or purging tendencies might occur, individuals might begin to count calories, log their food intake, and refuse to eat certain foods without any logical explanation. Their anxiety around food could lead them to develop strange eating patterns or rituals, such as skipping meals, chewing food to excess before swallowing, frequently denying that they are hungry, or eating but making frequent trips to the bathroom after meals. Some people develop strict exercise routines that if delayed, broken, or interfered with can provoke anger, depression, or anxiety.

Bingeing symptoms, on the other hand, are sometimes harder to spot because many perform this behavior when they are alone. However, signs of consumption in unreasonably large portions during very quick amounts of time, and with little self-control, can be alarming. Finding wrappers, food packaging, food being stored in odd places, or other evidence of excessive snacking can point toward bingeing.

When these diseases are further in development, physical signs may be more obvious. People suffering from anorexia will exhibit extreme weight loss during a very short time period. They might seem frequently cold, tired, or

It can be difficult to assess if a friend's behavior is veering into unhealthy territory. Excessive logging of food consumption can be a warning sign that something is wrong.

lethargic, and often their hair, skin, and nails can look dry and brittle due to lack of nutrition. Individuals who purge chronically may experience swelling around the mouth, stained teeth from excessive vomiting, and even develop rough patches of skin on their hands. Bingeing is an eating disorder that can be more difficult to detect physically. It can be more obvious through observation of behavior. However, people who binge can sporadically gain weight during episodes of overeating.

Eating disorders are often coupled with other symptoms that can affect mental health. Depression, isolation, anger, or anxiety can all be created, affected, or exacerbated by disordered eating.

THE INVISIBLE: EMOTIONAL

Different eating disorders have different emotional warning signs. These signs can sometimes be invisible or seem harder to notice. However, they share a few qualities. People with eating disorders are often also experiencing severe emotional issues that can manifest themselves in mental distress or illness. Isolation, depression, anxiety, acting out, or overachievement are sometimes ascribed to hormonal changes or "growing up," but these qualities can often also be the less visible partners of an eating disorder as well.

CONSEQUENCES OF EATING DISORDERS

If left unchecked, the effects of an eating disorder will wreak havoc on a person's body. Long-term complications can lead to dramatic health problems. Anorexia can lead to consequences such as heart failure, low bone density, kidney failure, and even death from starvation in the worst of cases. Likewise, bulimia and binge eating can have devastating effects. Chronic purging can result in tooth decay, ulcers, or gastric ruptures, and bingeing can promote high cholesterol, heart disease, and even diabetes.

CHAPTER THREE

I THINK MY FRIEND MAY HAVE AN EATING DISORDER. WHAT SHOULD I DO?

If you suspect that a friend might have an eating disorder, your might feel conflicted about how to react or move forward. There are so many options and none of them feel right. Eating disorders are serious business. Even if your suspicions are unconfirmed, you can address your fears without straining a friendship or making it awkward.

USING YOUR BEST JUDGMENT

First, consider how you might feel if you were in your friend's shoes. If you had a problem, would you want the whole world to know about it? Probably not. While it is important not to encourage someone's eating disorder by helping him or her to keep it secret, it is definitely not the best idea to speak openly about it to others before you have talked to your friend first—especially if there is a chance your concern might be misconstrued as gossip.

What about keeping it to yourself and hoping it will pass? While you may not want to seem nosy or inappropriate, this can be a dangerous idea. It is certainly possible that your friend may not have an eating disorder. However, something in his or her behavior set off your alarm bells. This may mean he or she might be going through some kind of stress that requires your support. Staying silent about your concerns may not give your friend the opportunity to tackle the problem before it becomes too big to handle.

But shouldn't you tell someone? His or her parents? A teacher? Someone who is equipped to handle this? Absolutely. But it is also important to consider that you may not have all the information. Telling your friend's parents before speaking with your friend can create an interpersonal mess. Your friend might get angry and view it as meddling, or resent you for putting him or her in a difficult position, especially without definitive proof of your suspicions.

Talking to a school counselor or a trusted adult is a healthy way to voice concerns about a friend's suspected eating disorder.

On the other hand, talking to a counselor or a trusted intermediary is a low-risk, high-reward path. Counselors are trained to deal with delicate situations and know when to intervene and when to wait. They are also confidential, so no one will know what you discuss. Addressing your concerns in private, it is important to give an honest assessment of your friend's condition. Your counselor can suggest a path forward while also considering further intervention.

THE IMPORTANCE OF EARLY INTERVENTION

Do you know the mental disorder with the highest mortality rate? The answer may surprise you: anorexia nervosa. According to the National Institutes of Mental Health (NIMH), about 10 percent of those who suffer from anorexia will die from the condition. Some die from starvation or metabolic collapse, and many die from suicide, which is higher among women suffering with anorexia than women with most other forms of mental disorder. The longer these disorders go unchecked, the harder they become to treat. Doctors stress that early intervention and treatment is crucial to a successful recovery. Habits are less ingrained, and it is easier to undo the destructive thinking that eating disorders thrive on. If you suspect a friend is developing an eating disorder, acting early can limit or even stop these conditions from becoming deathly problems.

At the end of the day, talking to your friend directly about your concerns is always the best place to start. It can seem like the least appealing option, but there are several ways you can prepare yourself for the conversation. It is very possible that your friend will feel relieved that someone has noticed his or her problem even if he or she reacts with a strong sense of denial, embarrassment, anger, or shame.

COMMITTING TO RESEARCH AND PREPARING RESOURCES

The most important thing you can do for your friend is to recommend professional help. No matter how much you may learn about eating disorders, you are not an expert on the topic and are not equipped to handle the problem alone. Using resources such as this one to educate yourself about eating disorders and how to handle them is a very crucial first step. But this should always be followed by extensive research into the resources your community offers a person with an eating disorder.

Although it can be tempting to offer an opinion about a friend's eating disorder, pointing him or her toward credible and trustworthy sources is the best thing you can do.

When browsing for more information online, be sure to visit official websites on the topic that offer the most up-to-date and accurate information. Personal blogs, social media accounts, and web forums can seem insightful, but they are not the best or the most precise sources of information. Government, state, and county health websites offer links to the mental health services available in your area. Official organizations such as NEDA and NIMH are filled to the brim with useful and practical information, advice, guides, and self-screening tests.

OBSERVING BEHAVIORS

Before talking with your friend, it might be a good idea to observe and take note of the behavior that concerned you. People suffering with eating disorders, especially those in earlier stages, grow very skilled at deflecting uncomfortable conversations or questions. Many sufferers might still be in denial, and others might be justifying their behavior to themselves and to others as a coping mechanism. Being able to offer a fixed example of a concerning situation can make it more difficult for the person suffering to continue using denial as a shield.

So what does observation entail, exactly? It does not mean that you should act like a babysitter or monitor what a friend eats, how a friend behaves, or where a friend goes. Simply being mindful of things that seem abnormal and taking special care to remember is enough.

WHAT IS THE BEST APPROACH? UNDERSTANDING YOUR ROLE

Deciding on the nature of your talk is an important thing to do before embarking on a discussion. Talking could mean a lot of things after all, and you might be surprised about how much thought needs to go into this interaction. Remember, eating disorders are very delicate subjects, and uncomfortable conversations can often seem to have a power dynamic. Your friend might feel ambushed, inferior, angry, scared, or blamed. This meeting should not be hostile or aggressive, however—think of it less like a confrontation and more like a conversation.

A conversation doesn't have to turn into a confrontation. Organizing your concerns and your advice beforehand will turn a difficult conversation into a reasoned discussion.

Author and psychologist Jeanne Albronda Heaton offers some advice in her book *Talking to Eating Disorders* about the importance of staying in your role. She warns that although it may be tempting to act outside of your limits—meaning to promise more than you can give, or exert more authority than you have—this can be dangerous not only for you but for your friend as well. Your friend might not be ready or responsive to your message or your concern if it voiced in a way that is outside of your relationship to him or her. The best thing you do when approaching your friend is to be honest and to act as a friend rather than something you are not.

10 GREAT QUESTIONS TO ASK A GUIDANCE COUNSELOR

1 WHAT ARE SOME SYMPTOMS OF EATING DISORDERS?

2 WHAT SHOULD I DO IF I THINK MY FRIEND MIGHT HAVE AN EATING DISORDER?

3 HOW CAN I HELP MY FRIEND SEE PAST BODY IMAGE?

4 HOW SHOULD I URGE MY FRIEND TO GET PROFESSIONAL HELP?

5 SHOULD I INVOLVE MY FRIEND'S PARENTS IN THE SITUATION?

6 WHAT ARE SOME GOOD RESOURCES THAT YOU CAN RECOMMEND TO ME?

7 DOES OUR SCHOOL OR LOCAL COMMUNITY HAVE PROGRAMS IN PLACE THAT ADDRESS EATING DISORDERS?

8 WHAT SHOULD I DO IF THERE ARE RUMORS GOING AROUND ABOUT MY FRIEND'S EATING DISORDER?

9 HOW DO I SUPPORT MY FRIEND WITHOUT OVERWHELMING MYSELF?

10 HOW CAN I ENCOURAGE MY FRIEND TO BELIEVE RECOVERY IS POSSIBLE?

CHAPTER FOUR

TALKING THE TALK: HOW TO APPROACH A FRIEND ABOUT AN EATING DISORDER

I t can feel intimidating to approach a friend about his or her disordered eating. Having a conversation with someone who has an eating disorder is very different from having a conversation with someone who does not. Certain words, phrases, and settings can act as triggers, complicating the interaction. It is normal to experience anxiety or fear about saying the wrong thing, but initiating a respectful dialogue with the friend in question is the best thing you can do for him or her. Understanding the nuances behind disordered eating is the key to learning how to talk about them.

WHAT'S ON THE AGENDA? PICKING A SETTING AND TIME

It might be tempting to address concerns during a casual conversation or in a public place. After all, it would take away the pressure from an official meeting and make the interaction seem less serious. However, it is important to

Two teens are having a serious discussion in private. Meeting like this makes them more likely to have a productive talk.

treat your concerns with the gravity they deserve. Picking a location that is quiet, private, and comfortable is pivotal to a productive conversation. If there is a chance of being interrupted or being distracted from the topic at hand, it can be easy for your friend to sweep it under the rug and continue ignoring the problem.

Timing is an equally important consideration. Remember, people who suffer from disordered eating experience high levels of anxiety or preoccupation around food. It is probably a good idea not to have your conversation over lunch or at a time when a meal usually occurs. Because eating disorders often have roots in other stresses, try not to pick a time that is especially busy or demanding either. Approaching a friend the week of a big test can create a domino effect of stress, making him or her less focused on the sincerity of your concerns.

Finally, also consider your friend's mood. Does he or she seem tired, irritable, sleepy? If so, it is probably a good idea to postpone the conversation until he or she is in a better, more receptive state. With all these considerations, it may seem difficult to find the right time to talk. However, knowing the time to avoid can make the difference between a productive interaction and a fruitless one.

WHAT KIND OF LANGUAGE SHOULD I USE?

Being mindful of language can feel odd when you are used to talking to a friend in a particular way. When talking about an eating disorder, it is better to make assertions and statements using the first person singular "I" rather than the second person address "you." When language such as "Why are you doing this to yourself?" or "You are scaring me" is used, it may seem to your friend that there is blame or judgment being leveled—and this can close the door of communication.

This does not mean that you should not express your concerns about the specific behavior you find alarming, of course. Your friend needs to hear examples of how his or her disorder eating is worrisome. Using first-person observation statements, such as "I am nervous about your behavior" or "I noticed that you lost a lot of weight," takes the responsibility of the feelings onto the speaker rather than the friend, which can make for a more productive conversation. When your friend feels like he or she is not being judged, then he or she will feel more inclined to share.

DIGGING DEEP: FOCUSING ON THE EMOTIONS BEHIND DISORDERED EATING

It can be easy to blurt out the things we are worried about the most. "Why aren't you eating?" or "Are you sure you should be eating this much?"— these are both valid concerns that may seem to get to the heart of the matter. It is important to remember that disordered eating is not really about food. You should address the behaviors that you find concerning, but the conversation should be focused on your friend's feelings and at getting to the bottom of what's caus-

Your body language has big impact on how your friend will receive your message. Similarly, be aware of what your friend's body language is telling you.

ing his or her stress, anxiety, or shame. The emotions and psychological issues he or she is experiencing contributed to the development of their disordered eating, so it makes sense to tackle these problems first. Asking the following questions can help your friend to open up about the issues they are experiencing:

I've noticed that you seem to have lost a lot of weight, but also that you seem to be very unhappy lately—can we talk about what's going on?

I feel like you might be going through something and that it is affecting your health. Can we discuss what's causing your anguish? I want to understand what you are feeling.

I've noticed that you seem kind of depressed lately, too. I know you've been spending a lot of time alone. I want to be there for you. Will you share what you are feeling with me?

REMAINING MINDFUL AND CONSIDERATE

When someone confides something with so much negative stigma attached to it, she or he is making herself or himself extremely vulnerable. It is good to keep this in mind when a friend shares with you the intimate details of her or his relationship to her or his disordered eating. Do not interrupt, dismiss, or invalidate your friend's feelings. Being a good listener is the best way to be considerate.

That being said, your friend may try to rationalize the behavior and explain why his or her obsessions are "not that bad." In this case, remember to remain mindful of the truth. As much as it may be easy to see a friend's point of view or sympathize with the struggle, do not support illogical thinking or irrational justifications. Endorsing, or giving approval, to such behavior might placate your friend for a time, but it will delay the necessary confrontation with the condition. Simply stating, "I see that you may feel that way, but I don't think that this behavior is healthy or normal" is enough to set the case straight. It is possible to be supportive without being combative or enabling.

HOW TO DEAL WITH YOUR FRIEND'S REACTIONS

Everybody deals with confrontation in different ways. Many people who have just begun to experience disordered eating may become defensive or angry, denying that the behavior is somehow abnormal. Another person might deflect or use denial, even if he or she knows that there is a problem. Often people suffering from these conditions think they have their behavior under control or can control it if they needed to. They might act stubbornly and insist that they can handle their own issues. Of course, there is always the possibility that an individual has been waiting for an opportunity to speak out about the problem. He or she may be subdued with despair, helplessness, or depression, and might react tearfully or emotionally.

Remember not to feed into anger, blame, or aggression. When dealing with severe emotions, the best thing to do is remain calm and reasonable, and listen to what is being said. If a conversation turns too heated, you should end it. It is not up to you to force your friend to admit a problem, nor is it your responsibility to help him or her rationalize unhealthy justifications. By having approached your friend, you have opened a door to help, and you have let him or her know that you are aware of the issue.

THE BEST ADVICE IS PROFESSIONAL ADVICE: ENCOURAGING YOUR FRIEND TO SEEK HELP

No matter how your friend responds to your concerns, it is best to encourage him or her to seek outside help. Wanting to give advice and help is natural—you care about your friend and want to be there to help—but only a medical or psychiatric professional is truly equipped to deal with the magnitude of an eating disorder. There are many ways that you can communicate this to a friend. Coming prepared with resources can be one of them. Printing a pamphlet, from reputable organizations such as NEDA and ANRAD, compiling a list of support groups in your community, or even providing your friend with a link to a self-screening test can be a push in the right direction to getting help.

THE DIFFERENCE BETWEEN PRIVACY AND SECRECY

Your friend might feel relieved that someone has finally picked up on his or her condition and begin to confide in you.

SPOTLIGHT ON SELF-SCREENING

If you are wondering where to direct a friend in need, a self-screening exam can often be a good starting point. Many people can be reluctant to admit that they have a problem in front of a friend or an audience. These exams allow individuals to participate in an anonymous quiz aimed at determining the degree and type of eating disorder one might be experiencing. They are free, anonymous, and can be taken online in the privacy of one's home. Self-screening exams, such as NEDA's test, can often serve as a tool of self-examination and push a person out of denial and into realization.

You might be asked to keep the disordered eating a "secret." It is understandable that an individual might not want the problems aired out in public. Being the object of gossip, speculation, or entertainment is a primary fear for many people who are affected by an eating disorder. However, what this friend is really asking for is privacy, not secrecy. Under no circumstance should you agree to keep your friend's issue a secret. This can enable his or her behavior. Making it clear to your friend that you respect the need for privacy and will not talk openly to others about the issue if prompted is OK. But also make sure to let your friend know that you will not help to hide his or her issue, especially if it continues to get worse.

REMAINING AWARE AND FOLLOWING UP

Eating disorders take time to develop, and they also take time to cure. You might hope that a conversation will somehow resolve a friend's eating disorder or prompt her or him to seek help right away. While this is a hopeful thought, it is not usually the case. Individuals often explore their options and feelings for a while before they are ready to receive help. This process might take some time. This does not mean, however, that your efforts were unsuccessful or a waste of time. Opening a dialogue with a friend is one of the best things that can be done for him or her, because it can provide the crucial first push toward self-examination.

Enlisting the help of a parent can be a daunting task. First, you must decide between your parents or your friend's.

It is important to continue observing your friend's behavior and to encourage him or her to get help. However, if the condition continues to worsen, contacting a parent, a teacher, or a counselor to intervene is not only appropriate but necessary. You have opened the door to a much-needed conversation, but sometimes it can take too long for someone to admit he or she needs help. Some people go their entire lives without admitting they have a problem. If your friend continues to exhibit dangerous behavior and refuses to get help, contact a responsible adult as soon as possible.

CHAPTER FIVE

TREATMENT, SUPPORT, AND RECOVERY

So, your friend has agreed to seek help. What next? Even if he or she might eventually join a support group or begin therapy, the journey ahead may still be far from over. Although it is not necessary to be personally involved in a friend's treatment program, being aware of what occurs in one can be helpful—especially if your friend has initial questions or concerns about what each approach entails.

THERAPY AND SUPPORT GROUPS

Seeking therapy for an eating disorder usually happens through a licensed psychiatrist. These medical professionals can offer support and care through psychological guidance and can also refer patients to qualified therapists. This kind of treatment is usually face-to-face and aimed at helping differentiate healthy eating habits from destructive ones, with an emphasis on developing a sense of positive body image through discussion.

Additionally, many support groups are available to help someone with disordered eating. Finding the right one will depend on the type of disorder the affected person

Healthcare professionals can formally diagnose a patient with an eating disorder, offer dietary guidance, treat with therapy, and facilitate other services to aid in recovery.

has. Support groups meet regularly and are available in the evenings or after school. Being part of a community in which recovery is a group effort can be incredibly effective for some individuals.

IN-PATIENT PROGRAMS

When disordered eating begins to become life-threatening, the person with the condition must be taken out of his or her everyday life. In-patient programs offer twenty-four-hour care and guided therapy for the mind and body. Counselors and psychiatrists create a regimen of care in the hospital, including medication if need be, to address coexisting psychological conditions. Often patients live and work with others who are also learning to understand their disorders. Before being discharged, doctors work with patients to devise an "action plan" to deal with everyday life.

IN THE SPOTLIGHT: DEMI LOVATO

Getting her start on the sets of Disney Channel movies such as *Camp Rock* and *Sonny with a Chance*, Demi Lovato is no stranger to growing up in the spotlight. The actress soon transitioned into a successful solo singing career, but her public struggles with depression, self-harm, and bulimia led her into a rehabilitation program in 2010. Since completing the program, Lovato has revealed to Katie Couric that she struggled with body image since the age of three, largely because of the way she felt she "should" look. Since then, she has been a vocal advocate of recovery and treatment for eating disorders. She frequently speaks out about damaging cultural perceptions of what bodies should look like and continues to be public about the importance of seeking treatment. "My words of encouragement to teen girls that are suffering from eating disorders, self-harm, anything, is to get help. That's the most important thing that you can do for yourself. It can change your life and potentially save your life."

MULTI-DISCIPLINARY APPROACHES

Some eating disorder specialists recommend a multi-disciplinary approach for treating eating disorders. Patients will have a team of advisers made up of psychiatrists, therapists, dieticians, and other supportive figures that work together to address all aspects of disordered eating. This, while extensive, can provide an individual with guidance on all fronts and help him or her to learn healthy habits for the mind, the body, and the spirit.

WHAT DO INCREMENTAL IMPROVEMENTS LOOK LIKE?

Eating disorder recovery is often slow, as it takes time for those affected to relearn what a healthy relationship with food should look like. You might wonder what signs indicate that your friend is on a better path. You might expect someone with anorexia to gain weight. You might also expect someone dealing with binge eating to lose weight in order to indicate that there is improvement, Often, however, negative thoughts and psychological trauma need to heal first. Positive adjustments to attitude, self-esteem, and seeming less anxious or guarded around food are signs of incremental recovery in the right direction.

COMBATTING GOSSIP AND BULLYING

For many people, knowing an acquaintance with an eating disorder can provoke gossip in a school or recreational setting. However, it is important to be mindful that gossip can be especially damaging to someone's recovery and set the person back. For a person with an eating disorder, gossip and verbal or physical bullying can magnify symptoms and self-awareness, which are linked closely with self-esteem. If you hear gossip or witness your friend being bullied, make sure to point out that it is inappropriate and cruel. Share your concerns with a teacher or school official so he or she can help come up with a plan to prevent further damage.

FOOD AND SOCIAL LIFE

As a friend, it is important to treat the person you care about with a sense of normalcy. Continue to invite them to social events, talk about things other than eating disorders, and enjoy activities together. One of the best things a person recovering from an eating disorder can do is find a hobby or activity that brings joy and removes the attention away from feelings and thoughts. Encouraging your friend to find interests or return some attention to things he or she used to love to do can be helpful. Activities such as arts and crafts, journaling, learning how to play an instrument, or participating in some kind of group activity are all great things to encourage your friend to do.

You might find yourself worried about how to approach situations related to food or exercise. After all, you can't avoid these things forever—and you shouldn't. It is important that you do not alter your behavior, your diet, or your routines in order to accommodate someone with an eating disorder. You may not want to eat in front of someone who is struggling with food, but you must continue to live your life normally. Creating specialized environments for someone can prevent him or her from learning to deal with real-life situations and conditions that he or she will have to overcome in order to get better.

STAYING CONNECTED: ENCOURAGEMENT AND SUPPORT

It can be challenging to offer encouragement because there can be anxiety about saying the wrong thing. When a friend is improving, it can be temping to say things like, "You look so much better!" To the average ear, this can seem like a compliment. But to a person recovering, body-focused comments

Everything is better with people who care about you. Making improvements in mental health and physical health will be much easier for your friend with a strong support system.

can mean a totally different thing. "You look healthy!" can easily translate to "I must look fat" when a person's self-image is still a work-in-progress.

Offering encouragement through positive, affirming statements that focus more on mood or encouragement are the way to go. "I am so proud of you," "It is so great to see you looking happier," or "You are being so brave" are great ways to indicate that you believe in your friend's recovery without referring to the physical. As much as it is important to encourage and support, be sure also not to feed into any negativity a person may have. If a friend says, "I look so awful," or "I feel like I'm getting nowhere," simply tell your friend that he or she is doing great and is on the right path.

RED FLAGS AND RELAPSES

It is normal to be concerned about a friend relapsing, or reverting back to disordered eating. Recovery, like any other complex process, can often have many ups and downs. If an individual has shown improvement but then suddenly begins to revert back to the same behavior that he or she exhibited during the development or low points of the eating disorder, a loved one has the right to be concerned. However, it is important to note the difference between an occasional slip-up and a relapse. Asking your friend feelings-based questions is one way to determine the difference. "Are you feeling stressed out?" or "Do you mind my asking how everything is going?" are good places to start.

If your friend claims that he or she is doing alright and is on track, respect this but continue to observe the behavior. If the disordered habits become more frequent than occasional, this is a red flag. Deviating from a medically prescribed diet, exhibiting a renewed interest in excessive exercising, avoiding food-related activities, increasing negative self-talk, or isolating oneself are all causes for concern when they become frequent and undeniable. Recovery is often a long journey that can take many years. If a friend is heading toward a relapse, the best, and most responsible, thing you can do is encourage him or her to seek help and let a trusted adult know.

Spotting a relapse is difficult because you won't witness every meal, or other aspects of your friend's struggle. Furthermore, it is easy to misinterpret signs as harmless behavior, and vice versa.

BEING A FRIEND TO YOURSELF: KNOWING YOUR LIMITS

It is easy to let apprehension and distress overtake your life when someone you love has an eating disorder. If thoughts and worries start to occupy your days, and it seems like there is little else to think about than your friend's eating disorder, it might be a good idea to step back and take some time off. While it is admirable to offer support and help, remember that being there for a friend does not mean that the condition should take over your life. You are not obligated to be an acting therapist or 24/7 crisis hotline. There are many ways you can help your friend without burning yourself out, and that can be achieved by setting boundaries and remembering that you also have interests and activities that you are allowed to enjoy and pursue on your own.

If you find yourself the recipient of unreasonable or frequent requests, it is OK to say, "I want to be there for you throughout this journey, and I appreciate the confidence you are putting in me, but right now, I need to focus on some things that are going on in my life. Can we talk about this again very soon?" or "I hope you understand that I care about you so much, but I need to take some time off today to handle a few things on my own."

UNDERSTANDING YOUR MENTAL HEALTH NEEDS

Likewise, it can be easy to get overwhelmed by the feelings experienced during this phase of your friend's life. Being supportive of a friend's eating disorder often entails hearing and dealing with many emotions and psychological trauma. Unfortunately, many people in this position often forget to take care of themselves. It is never a bad idea to schedule talks with a counselor or trusted adult to address your feelings about the situation, and to make sure that your mental health needs are taken care of as well. You cannot help your friend if you do not help yourself first.

The end of an eating disorder is the beginning of a better life. Being there for all of it is the greatest gift of friendship.

MOVING FORWARD TOGETHER

For people dealing with disordered eating, success is not always a linear process. Symptoms come and go and return. But friends do not. As a friend you can be there to support the one you care about. The truth is, a person with disordered eating can still go on to enjoy life, attend school, work toward a career, and plan a family, but the support of friends like you can bring the fruits of life closer to hand.

GLOSSARY

AMERICAN PSYCHIATRIC ASSOCIATION (APA) An organization of professional psychiatrists; the association publishes the *DSM-5*.

ANOREXIA NERVOSA Extreme weight loss, often achieved through self-imposed starvation.

BINGEING Excessive food consumption in a short period of time.

BMI Short for body mass index, a formula used by medical professionals to determine healthy weight ranges for individuals.

BULIMIA NERVOSA Eating in excessive quantities, usually followed by purging.

COMPENSATORY Any action taken to balance out or make up for a previous action.

COMPULSIVE EXERCISE Excessive exercising often utilized by people with eating disorders to make up for feelings of shame or guilt associated with eating.

DIAGNOSTIC AND STATISTICAL MANUAL OF MENTAL DISORDERS (DSM-5) The standard manual for the classification of mental disorders used by mental health professionals in the United States.

DIETICIAN A licensed professional equipped to dispense expert advice on an individual's diet and nutritional needs.

DIURETIC A drug used to force or increase urination.

FAD DIET A diet that is trendy but has no basis in medical fact.

FASTING Abstaining from food or drink for an extended period of time.

FMRI Short for functional magnetic resonance imaging, a computer program that scans the brain for blood flow and activity.

LAXATIVE A drug used to stimulate bowel movements.

OSFED Short for other specified feeding or eating disorders; an eating disorder that does not meet the diagnosing criteria for anorexia nervosa, bulimia nervosa, or binge eating disorder.

PSYCHIATRIST A medical professional who diagnoses and treats mental illness.

PURGING Self-induced vomiting, often a symptom of bulimia nervosa.

RELAPSE A state of regression after improvements have been made.

RESTRICTION Severely limiting calorie intake, often to the point of starvation.

STIGMA Shame that is associated with a circumstance or behavior.

FOR MORE INFORMATION

The Alliance for Eating Disorders Awareness
1649 Forum Place #2
West Palm Beach, FL 33401
Helpline: (866) 662-1235
Website: http://www.allianceforeatingdisorders.com/portal/home
The Alliance for Eating Disorders Awareness offers free pre-
   sentations about eating disorders, free assistance in seeking
   resources for treatment, and a toll-free hotline.

Binge Eating Disorder Association (BEDA)
637 Emerson Place
Severna Park, MD 21146
Hotline: (855) 855-2332
Website: http://bedaonline.com
BEDA provides recommended reading on the topic of eating
   disorders, a resource guide for treatment options, and a friends
   and family toolkit. Call BEDA's helpline if you have any questions about how to help someone with a binge eating disorder.

Eating Disorders Foundation of Canada
Suite 230A, 100 Collip Circle
Research Park, Western University
London, ON N6G 4X8
Canada
Helpline: (519) 858-5111
Website: http://www.edfofcanada.com
Eating Disorders Foundation of Canada connects community
   groups with the resources they need to make eating disorder
   awareness and prevention more visible and accessible. Their
   "outside links" section provides a wide directory of resources
   and treatment centers across Canada.

National Association of Anorexia Nervosa and Associated
  Disorders (ANAD)
750 E. Diehl Road #127
Naperville, IL 60563
Hotline: (630) 577-1330
Email: anadhelp@anad.org
Website: http://www.anad.org
Anorexia Nervosa and Associated Disorders (ANAD) specializes
  in answering questions regarding eating disorders and locating
  professional resources in your area. Its website offers links to
  counselors across the country, as well as support programs.

National Eating Disorders Association (NEDA)
165 West 46th Street, Suite 402
New York, NY 10036
Hotline: (800) 931-2237
Website: http://www.nationaleatingdisorders.org
Visit the National Eating Disorders Association (NEDA) website for a wealth of information, including in-depth studies on
  the effects of eating disorders on teens, screening resources,
  and links to other professional organizations.

The National Eating Disorder Information Centre (NEDIC)
ES 7-421, 200 Elizabeth Street
Toronto, ON M5G 2C4
Canada
Helpline: (866) 633-4220
Website: http://nedic.ca
NEDIC offers information on prevention and treatment, and
  a thorough guide for friends and family with tips on how to
  approach their loved one about an eating disorder.

WEBSITES

Because of the changing nature of internet links, Rosen Publishing has developed an online list of websites related to the subject of this book. This site is updated regularly. Please use this link to access the list:

http://www.rosenlinks.com/HCIH/eat

FOR FURTHER READING

Dunkle, Clare, and Elena Dunkle. *Elena Vanishing: A Memoir.* San Francisco, CA: Chronicle Books, 2015.

Foran, Racquel. *Living with Eating Disorders* (Living with Health Challenges). Minneapolis, MN: ABDO Publishing Company, 2014.

Goldsmith, Connie. *Dietary Supplements: Harmless, Helpful, or Hurtful?* Minneapolis, MN: Twenty-First Century Books, 2016.

Taylor, Julia V. *The Body Image Workbook for Teens: Activities to Help Girls Develop Healthy Body Image in an Image-Obsessed World.* Oakland, CA: New Harbinger Publications, 2014.

Watson, Lucy, and Bryan Lask. *Can I Tell You About Eating Disorders?* (Can I Tell You About...?). Philadelphia, PA: Jessica Kingsley Publishers, 2014.

Watson, Stephanie, and Nita Mallick. *Conquering Binge Eating* (Conquering Eating Disorders). New York, NY: Rosen Publishing Group, 2016.

Watson, Stephanie, and Tammy Laser. *Eating Disorders* (Girls' Health). New York, NY: Rosen Publishing Group, 2011.

Willet, Edward, and Viola Jones. *Conquering Negative Body Image* (Conquering Eating Disorders). New York, NY: Rosen Publishing Group, 2016.

Williams, Kara, and Nicholas Faulkner. *Conquering Diet Drug Abuse* (Conquering Eating Disorders). New York, NY: Rosen Publishing Group, 2016.

Zahensky, Barbara, and Isobel Towne. *Conquering Fad Diet Fixation* (Conquering Eating Disorders). New York, NY: Rosen Publishing Group, 2016.

BIBLIOGRAPHY

Academy for Eating Disorders. "Eating Disorder Not Otherwise Specified (ED-NOS) or Feeding or Eating Disorders Not Elsewhere Classified (FED-NEC)." April 15, 2014 (http://www. aedweb.org/index.php/education/eating-disorder-information/ eating-disorder-information-2#AFRID).

American Psychiatric Association, *DSM-5*. "Feeding and Eating Disorders." May 27, 2013 (http://www.dsm5.org/documents/ eating%20disorders%20fact%20sheet.pdf).

Beating Eating Disorders. "Worried About Someone—How to Talk to Somebody." Retrieved March 15, 2016 (https://www.b-eat.co.uk/about-eating-disorders/worried-about-someone/how-to-talk-to-somebody).

Binge Eating Disorder Association. "The Recovery Process." Retrieved March 15, 2016 (http://bedaonline.com/understanding-binge-eating-disorder/recovery-process/).

Eating Disorder Hope. "Orthorexia, Excessive Exercise & Nutrition." January 31, 2014 (http://www.eatingdisorderhope. com/information/orthorexia-excessive-exercise).

Eating Disorders Coalition. "Facts About Eating Disorders— What the Research Shows." Retrieved March 18, 2016 (http:// eatingdisorderscoalition.org.s208556.gridserver.com/couch/ uploads/file/fact-sheet_2016.pdf).

Ellin, Abbey. "In Fighting Anorexia, Recovery Is Elusive." *New York Times*, April 25, 2011 (http://www.nytimes. com/2011/04/26/health/26anorexia.html?_r=0).

Families Empowered and Supporting Treatment of Eating Disorders. "Understanding ED Treatment." Retrieved March 13, 2016 (http://www.feast-ed.org/?page=TreatingEDs).

Hill, Laura. "Eating Disorders from the Inside Out." TEDx
  Columbus, 2012 (http://tedxcolumbus.com/speakers-per-
  formers/2012-the-future-revealed-speakers-performers/
  laura-hill-phd/).

National Association of Anorexia Nervosa and Associated Disorders. "How to Help Someone—How to Help."
  Retrieved March 18, 2016 (http://www.anad.org/wp-content/
  uploads/2016/02/How-to-Help-2016.pdf).

National Eating Disorder Information Centre. "Reflections on
  Genes and Eating Disorders." 2005 (http://nedic.ca/node/827).

National Eating Disorders Association. "Contributing Factors &
  Prevention." Retrieved March 15, 2016 (http://www.nationale-
  atingdisorders.org/contributing-factors-prevention).

National Eating Disorders Association. "Diversity Issues."
  Retrieved March 15, 2016 (http://www.nationaleatingdisor-
  ders.org/diversity).

National Eating Disorders Association. "Toolkits—Educator
  Toolkit." Retrieved March 16, 2016 (http://www.nationale-
  atingdisorders.org/toolkits).

Strauss, Claudia J., and Jeanne Albronda Heaton. *Talking
  to Eating Disorders: Simple Ways to Support Someone with
  Anorexia, Bulimia, Binge Eating, or Body Image Issues.* New
  York, NY: Penguin Publishing, 2005.

INDEX

ABOUT THE AUTHOR

Sabrina Parys is an author and editor living in Portland, Oregon. She holds an MA in book publishing from Portland State University. Following struggles with disordered eating in her youth, Parys became invested in learning about prevention and recovery through professional and educational resources. She hopes that her work will encourage young adults to become aware of the prevalence of eating disorders in their everyday lives. Parys enjoys hiking, reading, and learning more about translation in literature.

PHOTO CREDITS

Cover, p. 18 Syda Productions/Shutterstock.com; p. 5 SW Productions/Photodisc/Getty Images; p. 8 Markus Moellenberg/Corbis/Getty Images; p. 12 Yulia Reznikov/Shutterstock.com; p. 14 Master1305/Shutterstock.com; p. 23 rezart/iStock/Thinkstock; p. 24 Moodboard/Cultura/Getty Images; p. 27 Rob Marmion/Shutterstock.com; p. 29 hjalmeida/iStock/Thinkstock; p. 31 marekuliasz/iStock/Thinkstock; p. 35 Huy Lam/First Light/Getty Images; p. 37 Corbis/VCG/Getty Images; p. 42 SW Productions/Photodisc/Getty Images; p. 45 Tetra Images/Getty Images; p. 49 Hero Images/Getty Images; p. 51 BananaStock/Thinkstock; p. 53 Klaus Vedfelt/DigitalVision/Getty Images; cover and interior pages background images © iStockphoto.com/chaluk.

Designer: Brian Garvey; Photo Researcher: Sherri Jackson; Editor: Bernadette Davis